Preface

This book embarks on an exploration of the intricate history of mental health care. From ancient beliefs in demonic possession and the practice of exorcism to the curious science of phrenology, it delves into a rich tapestry of historical interventions. It unravels paradoxes, such as moral confinement's well-intentioned care intersecting with the limits of knowledge. The book uncovers extremes in medical practices, explores the eerie specter of insulin-induced comas, and revisits the ancient procedure of trephination. It navigates the transformation of early psychosurgery into modern neurosurgery and traces the evolution of electroconvulsive therapy (ECT). This book mirrors human understanding, empathy, and compassion in the pursuit of answers to the profound questions surrounding mental illness.

Introduction

The annals of medical history are a testament to the enduring quest to understand, treat, and alleviate the complex and enigmatic nature of mental illnesses. The stories of individuals who grappled with psychological disorders throughout the ages are woven with narratives of resilience, perseverance, and the relentless pursuit of relief.

In this comprehensive exploration, we embark on a journey through the pages of time, tracing the remarkable and often bewildering array of interventions used to address mental illness. From the ancient beliefs that attributed mental disturbances to demonic possession, leading to the practice of exorcism, to the intricacies of trephination, which involved the surgical removal of a circular piece of skull, these interventions reflect the evolving knowledge, beliefs, and medical practices of their eras.

The chapters of this book take us through the realms of history, revealing practices that range from the bizarre and cruel to the deeply humane and well-intentioned. We delve into the origins of phrenology, an elaborate pseudoscience that claimed to read personality traits from the contours of the skull. We explore the shadowy world of psychosurgery, where early forms of lobotomies involved physically altering the brain in an attempt to treat mental illness, often with severe side effects.

The pages turn, and we encounter the more curious and imaginative interventions, such as the mesmerism that involved the use of magnets or hypnosis to treat various ailments, including mental health conditions, which has long been discredited as pseudoscience. From the tranquilizer chair that immobilized agitated individuals to the agonizing blisters created to draw out "bad humors" believed to be the cause of mental illness, we peel back the layers of history to reveal the contrasting and sometimes harrowing approaches to mental health care.

We also explore the compassionate yet limited concept of moral confinement, which involved confining individuals with mental illness in structured and supportive environments. It marked a shift towards more humane care, even as it is seen as outdated due to its constraints. Throughout this odyssey, we uncover the enduring debate surrounding the controversial practice of exorcism, where mental illness was often attributed to demonic possession, leading to rituals intended to expel malevolent forces.

We revisit the early 20th-century beliefs that transfusing blood from "healthy" individuals could cure psychiatric disorders and the subsequent development of insulin-induced comas as treatments for conditions like schizophrenia, both practices that have since been discredited. The story of bloodletting unfolds as we witness the belief in removing "bad blood" as a treatment for mental disturbances, which eventually gave way to more modern medical practices and knowledge.

We peer into the world of trephination, an ancient surgical procedure that involved the removal of a circular piece of skull and was used for a range of medical, cultural, and ritualistic purposes. And then, we arrive at the evolution of electroconvulsive therapy (ECT), a controversial treatment that has been refined and adapted to contemporary ethical standards.

As we navigate the complex landscape of historical interventions for mental illness, we encounter a broad spectrum of beliefs, practices, and intentions. Some of these interventions were born out of desperation, a lack of scientific understanding, or the influence of deeply ingrained cultural and religious beliefs. Others were well-intentioned attempts to alleviate suffering and provide solace to individuals experiencing the harrowing journey of mental illness.

While many of these practices are now considered obsolete, their legacies endure, and they serve as a testament to the enduring commitment of humanity to confront and understand the intricate challenges posed by mental disorders. The journey through these pages offers not only a glimpse into the past but also a mirror through which to reflect on the evolution of mental health care, the ethical considerations that guide it, and the enduring search for effective and compassionate treatments.

1. Rotational Therapy

In the annals of medical history, we can find some truly bizarre and often cruel interventions used in the treatment of mental health conditions. These archaic practices, devoid of scientific basis and filled with misplaced good intentions, frequently did more harm than good. One such treatment that stands as a chilling testament to the dark ages of mental health care is Rotational Therapy.

The 18th and 19th centuries were characterized by a pervasive lack of understanding about the complexities of mental illness. This was an era when asylums were overcrowded and patients were often subjected to inhumane conditions. Physicians were desperate to find ways to cure or at least alleviate the suffering of the mentally ill. This desperation gave birth to a wide array of treatments that ranged from the unusual to the downright macabre.

Rotational Therapy, at its core, was a method based on the belief that imbalances in the brain were responsible for mental illness. Physicians of the time theorized that by spinning patients at high speeds, they could restore balance to the brain and, in turn, cure them of their mental ailments. This theory, of course, was entirely unfounded, but it was pursued with a zealous determination that is difficult to comprehend today.

The apparatus used for Rotational Therapy was a menacing, wooden contraption, reminiscent of a torture device rather than a medical instrument. Patients were strapped into a chair that was mounted on a rotating platform, and this chair would then be set into a vigorous spin, akin to a human centrifuge. It was believed that the centrifugal force generated by the spinning motion would somehow realign the patient's brain, returning them to sanity.

The actual procedure was not only horrifying but also highly dangerous. Patients were subjected to forces that could lead to dizziness, nausea, and, in severe cases, injury. They were often forced into these devices against their will, restrained by leather straps, and subjected to the spinning motion until they were utterly exhausted or sometimes even unconscious. The rationalization behind this cruelty was the hope that it would force the demons of madness out of the patient's mind.

One of the most well-known proponents of Rotational Therapy was Dr. Benjamin Rush. He was a prominent American physician who signed the Declaration of Independence and later became known as the "Father of American Psychiatry." Dr. Rush had good intentions, seeking a way to alleviate the suffering of those with mental illnesses. However, his approach to Rotational Therapy, which he called the "gyrating chair," was nothing short of cruel.

In his book "Medical Inquiries and Observations," published in 1789, Dr. Rush described his rationale for Rotational Therapy, writing, "The best method of preventing or curing a maniacal or melancholic state of mind is to remove the disease in its commencement by the loss of a few ounces of blood and by purging." But if these initial measures failed, he advocated the use of the gyrating chair, believing it to be the only solution for "established mania."

Dr. Rush's advocacy for Rotational Therapy was not without its critics. In Europe, the approach was met with skepticism and scorn. Dr. Philippe Pinel, a French psychiatrist renowned for his humane treatment of the mentally ill, vocally opposed Rotational Therapy and other harsh treatments. Pinel argued that mental illness was not the result of imbalances in the brain that could be corrected by spinning. On the contrary, it was a complex interplay of environmental, genetic, and psychological factors.

Unfortunately, the American medical community at the time did not heed the warnings of their European counterparts. Rotational Therapy was used extensively in asylums across the United States, subjecting countless individuals to this nightmarish ordeal. Patients endured the horrors of the gyrating chair, often without any improvement in their condition and frequently with physical and psychological trauma.

It wasn't until the mid-19th century that Rotational Therapy began to fall out of favor. The field of psychiatry advanced and a more compassionate understanding of mental illness emerged. Treatments like the gyrating chair were gradually abandoned in favor of more humane and evidence-based approaches. The advent of psychotherapy and the use of psychoactive medications marked a turning point in the treatment of mental health conditions.

Looking back, it is difficult to fathom the cruelty and ignorance that underpinned Rotational Therapy and similar interventions. These treatments may have been born from a sincere desire to help those suffering from mental illness. However, they serve as a stark reminder of the dangers of medical practices based on unfounded theories and desperation.

Today, mental health care has come a long way, with a greater emphasis on compassion, evidence-based treatments, and respect for the dignity of every individual. The dark history of Rotational Therapy is a chilling cautionary tale.It reminds us of the harm that can be inflicted when we abandon reason and humanity in our quest to alleviate the suffering of the mentally ill.

In the end, the legacy of Rotational Therapy is one of suffering, but it also serves as a testament to the resilience of humanity. It reminds us of the importance of continually striving for a better understanding of mental health and seeking treatments that are not only effective but also rooted in compassion and respect for the inherent dignity of every individual.

2. Metrazol Therapy

Metrazol Therapy involved the administration of a drug called Metrazol to induce seizures in an attempt to cure conditions like schizophrenia and depression. This therapy gained notoriety in the early 20th century, highlighting a time when the understanding of mental health was limited. It also signifies how the pursuit of treatments sometimes led to unexpected and harrowing consequences.

The early 20th century marked a significant shift in the field of psychiatry. Emerging scientific theories and pharmaceutical developments held the promise of unlocking the secrets of the human mind and providing novel treatments for mental illnesses. Among these promising innovations was Metrazol, a synthetic drug with the peculiar ability to induce seizures.

Metrazol, also known as pentylenetetrazol, was initially developed as a circulatory stimulant. Its stimulating effects on the central nervous system led some psychiatrists to believe that it might offer a breakthrough in the treatment of mental disorders. The idea was that inducing seizures with Metrazol could "reset" the brain, effectively erasing or mitigating the symptoms of various mental illnesses.

The practice of Metrazol Therapy was not for the faint of heart. Patients subjected to this treatment were administered the drug intravenously or intramuscularly, causing them to experience intense seizures. These seizures were characterized by violent convulsions, loss of consciousness, and often resulted in temporary memory loss. The idea was that these seizures might, in some inexplicable way, alleviate the symptoms of conditions like schizophrenia, depression, and bipolar disorder.

The procedure itself was harrowing. Patients would be restrained, often with leather straps, to prevent injury during their violent convulsions. As they received the Metrazol injection, they would experience an almost immediate onset of a seizure. Their bodies would contort and thrash, creating a disturbing spectacle for the medical staff and family members who might be present. The experience was both physically and emotionally traumatic for the patients.

The proponents of Metrazol Therapy argued that the induced seizures could provide relief for patients suffering from mental disorders, offering a clean slate for their troubled minds. This belief was rooted in the early 20th-century understanding of mental illness. It often viewed these conditions as disturbances in the brain that could be "shocked" back to normalcy.

Dr. Ladislas J. Meduna, a Hungarian psychiatrist, was one of the leading advocates of Metrazol Therapy. He is credited with popularizing the treatment in the United States during the 1930s. Dr. Meduna fervently believed that seizures induced by Metrazol had a profound, curative effect on mental disorders. In his mind, Metrazol Therapy was a revolutionary advancement in psychiatric treatment.

The widespread adoption of Metrazol Therapy was facilitated by the limitations of available treatments at the time. Prior to the advent of psychoactive medications, options for treating mental illness were limited, and the quality of care in psychiatric hospitals left much to be desired. The suffering of patients and their families led to a desperate search for alternatives, making Metrazol Therapy. It was an appealing prospect for both medical professionals and those affected by mental illness.

While Metrazol Therapy was met with initial enthusiasm, it also generated substantial controversy and opposition. Many in the medical community were skeptical of its effectiveness and concerned about the potential harm it could cause to patients. The procedure itself was physically brutal and traumatizing, often resulting in injuries such as fractures and dislocated joints. The seizures induced by Metrazol could lead to postictal confusion and memory loss, leaving patients in a disoriented and vulnerable state.

Moreover, the ethical concerns surrounding Metrazol Therapy were mounting. The administration of a drug to induce seizures without the informed consent of patients raised serious ethical questions. Informed consent, a cornerstone of modern medical ethics, was not a standard practice in the early 20th century. As a result, many patients underwent Metrazol Therapy without a full understanding of the procedure's potential risks and benefits.

As time passed, Metrazol Therapy became increasingly controversial and was eventually replaced by less traumatic and more effective treatments. This included the development of psychoactive medications, such as lithium for bipolar disorder and the first-generation antipsychotics for schizophrenia. It marked a turning point in the treatment of mental illness.

These medications offered relief from symptoms without the need for physically traumatic interventions.

Metrazol Therapy gradually fell out of favor, but its legacy left a lasting impact on the history of psychiatric treatment. The controversies surrounding the practice and its associated risks helped pave the way for a more ethical and humane approach to mental health care. Informed consent and ethical treatment guidelines became standard practices in the field of psychiatry, ensuring that patients were treated with dignity and respect.

Today, the history of Metrazol Therapy serves as a stark reminder of the evolving nature of psychiatric care. While the intentions of those who advocated for the treatment may have been rooted in a genuine desire to help those suffering from mental illness, it underscores the importance of subjecting medical practices to rigorous scrutiny and ethical considerations.

The field of psychiatry has come a long way since the days of Metrazol Therapy. Contemporary mental health care emphasizes a holistic approach that combines psychotherapy, pharmacotherapy, and supportive interventions. The ethical principles that guide the treatment of mental illness have evolved to prioritize patient autonomy, informed consent, and the well-being of individuals living with mental disorders.

The story of Metrazol Therapy is a chilling reminder of the dark and sometimes misguided history of psychiatric treatment. It is a testament to the resilience of individuals living with mental illness, the dedication of medical professionals in the field of psychiatry, and the imperative of upholding ethical standards in the quest to alleviate human suffering. As we look back on this unsettling chapter in the history of mental health care, we are reminded that progress often arises from a critical examination of the past. We also learn the need for a commitment to compassionate, evidence-based, and ethical approaches to the treatment of mental illness.

3. Forced Vomiting

Forced vomiting was based on the belief that mental illness was caused by toxins in the body. This practice, which seems almost archaic by modern standards, serves as a chilling reminder of the dark and often tragic history of mental health care. The concept of toxins causing mental illness was not a novel one in the annals of medical history. It had its roots in ancient medical theories that posited an intricate connection between the body and the mind. This notion held that physical impurities and imbalances within the body could manifest as mental disorders. Therefore, in order to treat the mind, it was believed that one must first cleanse the body.

One of the most prevalent methods used to purge the body of these perceived toxins was forced vomiting. This practice was often carried out in a variety of ways, and it typically involved the administration of emetics—substances that induce vomiting. The aim was to expel the presumed impurities from the body through the act of vomiting, thereby relieving the patient of their mental afflictions.

Forced vomiting as a treatment for mental illness was particularly popular in the 18th and 19th centuries. During this era, medical understanding of mental illness was in its infancy, and treatments were often rooted in theories that appear astonishingly misguided in hindsight. The common practice of forced vomiting was based on a blend of ancient medical wisdom, contemporary beliefs, and a desire to find solutions for individuals suffering from mental disorders.

The methods used for forced vomiting varied, but they all shared a common objective: to induce the patient to vomit. Some practitioners administered emetics orally, while others employed more invasive procedures, such as the insertion of emetic substances through the nasal passages. The intent was to forcefully expel any perceived toxins from the patient's body, with the belief that doing so would alleviate their mental distress.

The physical and emotional toll exacted on patients subjected to forced vomiting was severe. The process of inducing vomiting was both uncomfortable and distressing. It often led to violent retching, abdominal pain, and a general feeling of helplessness. Patients were forced to endure these procedures in the belief that it would cleanse them of the toxins responsible for their mental suffering.

The theory behind forced vomiting was not entirely without basis, as it was rooted in the ancient principle of humorism. In humorism, it was believed that the body's health and mental state were governed by the balance of four bodily humors: blood, phlegm, black bile, and yellow bile. Mental illness was thought to result from an imbalance of these humors, and forced vomiting was seen as a way to restore equilibrium.

In the 18th and 19th centuries, some medical practitioners embraced this theory, and forced vomiting became a common treatment for mental disorders. However, the effectiveness of these procedures in relieving mental suffering was highly questionable. Many patients experienced no improvement, and some even saw their conditions worsen due to the physical and emotional distress caused by forced vomiting.

One of the most well-known proponents of forced vomiting was Dr. Benjamin Rush. He was not only an advocate for this method but also an early advocate for Rotational Therapy, as mentioned in a previous story. Dr. Rush believed that various forms of purging, including forced vomiting, could help restore the balance of humors and, by extension, cure mental disorders.

In his book "Medical Inquiries and Observations," published in 1789, Dr. Rush promoted the use of emetics and other purgatives as treatments for mental illness. He wrote, "The deranged action of the intestines is an effect of diseased sensibility of the nerves of the bowels... and these again are frequently affected by a sympathy with the nerves of the brain." In his view, forced vomiting and purging could influence these nerves and ultimately improve mental health.

While some physicians, like Dr. Rush, believed in the potential benefits of forced vomiting, there was growing skepticism about its effectiveness and ethical implications. Critics argued that the procedures were not only physically distressing but also carried significant risks, including dehydration and damage to the esophagus and stomach. The moral and ethical concerns surrounding the practice were also mounting, as patients were often subjected to these procedures without their informed consent.

Forced vomiting as a treatment for mental illness began to decline in the late 19th and early 20th centuries as the field of psychiatry advanced and began to adopt more humane and evidence-based practices. The emergence of psychotherapy and the development of psychoactive medications marked a significant shift in the treatment of mental disorders.

Today, we look back on the history of forced vomiting as a reminder of the remarkable progress that has been made in the field of mental health care. The ethical concerns and physical suffering associated with this practice have contributed to the development of more humane and compassionate approaches to the treatment of mental illness.

The story of forced vomiting is a sobering example of the dangers of medical practices based on unsubstantiated theories and a lack of understanding of mental illness. It highlights the importance of continually reevaluating and advancing the field of psychiatry to ensure that individuals living with mental disorders receive the most effective and compassionate care possible.

In modern mental health care, the emphasis is on evidence-based treatments, psychotherapy, and the use of medications with demonstrated efficacy. Ethical principles, such as informed consent and patient autonomy, are foundational to the practice of psychiatry. They ensure that individuals are treated with the respect and dignity they deserve.

As we reflect on the history of forced vomiting, we are reminded that the field of mental health care has come a long way. It was driven by a commitment to scientific progress, ethical principles, and the unwavering goal of alleviating the suffering of those living with mental illness.

4. Therapeutic Fasting

Therapeutic fasting involved prolonged periods of abstaining from food with the belief that it would purify the body and mind. The history of therapeutic fasting serves as a testament to the limitations of medical understanding and the often misguided quest for solutions to complex mental health challenges. It was rooted in ancient medical traditions, and was based on the belief that various physical and mental ailments could be cured or alleviated by abstaining from food. Proponents of therapeutic fasting argued that the act of fasting would cleanse the body of toxins, restore balance, and, in doing so, address the underlying causes of mental illness.

Fasting as a method of healing has a long history, with roots in the practices of ancient cultures, including the ancient Egyptians, Greeks, and Romans. It was often seen as a means to achieve spiritual purification and was associated with various religious and philosophical traditions. In the context of mental health treatment, therapeutic fasting began to gain traction in the late 19th and early 20th centuries. During this period, medical understanding of mental illness was still in its nascent stages, and the treatment options available were limited. Desperate for solutions, physicians and alternative healers turned to unconventional practices like therapeutic fasting.

The rationale behind therapeutic fasting was based on the notion that mental disorders were often the result of impurities in the body, which could be expelled through fasting. This perspective was influenced by ancient humoral theories of medicine, which posited that the body's health was dependent on the balance of bodily fluids, or "humors." An imbalance of humors was believed to lead to various physical and mental ailments.

It was argued that fasting could facilitate the removal of these impurities, thereby restoring the harmony necessary for mental well-being. The logic behind this approach was that by depriving the body of food, it would be forced to consume its own accumulated waste, ridding itself of toxins in the process.

Fasting, as a mental health treatment, took on several forms. Patients were often subjected to prolonged periods without food, sometimes lasting for several weeks. Some practitioners advocated for water-only fasts, while others permitted limited dietary intake, such as fruit juices or broths. The specific regimen and duration of fasting varied among practitioners, making it difficult to establish a standard approach.

The physical and psychological toll of therapeutic fasting was profound. Patients undergoing extended periods of fasting experienced extreme weakness, lethargy, and malnutrition. Prolonged fasting could lead to significant weight loss, and in some cases, it resulted in life-threatening complications, including cardiac arrhythmias and organ failure. The emotional and psychological distress of starvation, combined with the already challenging experience of mental illness, added to the suffering of patients subjected to this treatment.

One of the most prominent proponents of therapeutic fasting in the early 20th century was Dr. Linda Hazzard. She was an American physician who advocated for prolonged fasting as a means of curing various ailments, including mental illness. Dr. Hazzard claimed that fasting could heal not only the body but also the mind. Her controversial views and methods drew both attention and criticism.

Dr. Hazzard's approach to therapeutic fasting, however, was marked by ethical and legal controversies. She was known to have engaged in practices that were not only medically dubious but also highly unethical. She is infamously associated with cases in which patients died while under her care. These events raised concern about her competence and the safety of therapeutic fasting.

The widespread use of therapeutic fasting as a treatment for mental illness began to decline in the mid-20th century. As medical understanding of mental disorders advanced and new treatments emerged, the practice of fasting was increasingly seen as outdated and potentially harmful. The advent of psychoactive medications and the development of psychotherapy revolutionized the field of mental health care. It provided more effective and evidence-based treatments for individuals with mental illnesses.

Therapeutic fasting for mental health treatment has largely been abandoned. However, the historical use of this method remains a sobering reminder of the desperate and misguided attempts to address mental illness in the past. The suffering and risks associated with therapeutic fasting underscore the importance of evidence-based practices, ethical standards, and informed consent in the field of mental health care.

Modern mental health care has evolved to emphasize a holistic approach that combines psychotherapy, pharmacotherapy, and supportive interventions. Ethical principles, such as informed consent, patient autonomy, and the well-being of individuals living with mental disorders, are now central to psychiatric practice, ensuring that patients are treated with respect and dignity.

As we reflect on the history of therapeutic fasting, we are reminded of the progress that has been made in the field of mental health care. It underscores the importance of continuously reassessing and advancing our understanding of mental illness and the development of compassionate, evidence-based, and ethical approaches to treatment.

The story of therapeutic fasting is a testament to the resilience of individuals living with mental illness and the dedication of medical professionals in the field of psychiatry. It also reflects the necessity of upholding ethical standards in the pursuit of alleviating human suffering. It highlights the imperative of always seeking the most humane and effective treatments for mental disorders, guided by the principles of empathy, evidence, and ethical responsibility.

5. Tranquilizer Chair

The Tranquilizer Chair was a contraption designed to immobilize patients with restraints for extended periods with the intent of calming agitated individuals. This method, which seems inhumane by modern standards, serves as a chilling testament to the dark and often troubling history of mental health care.

The use of the Tranquilizer Chair dates back to the 19th century, a period marked by the widespread misunderstanding of mental illnesses and the limited treatment options available. During this time, the prevailing theories about mental disorders often centered on the belief that agitation and restlessness were symptoms of "madness." In the absence of effective treatments, patients who exhibited agitated behavior were often subjected to various forms of restraint.

The Tranquilizer Chair, as a concept, was based on the idea that immobilizing a patient would help restore calmness and order to their mind. It was designed to physically constrain individuals, often with leather or fabric restraints, rendering them immobile. The intent was to prevent the patient from engaging in agitated or violent behaviors, with the belief that forced immobilization would help alleviate their mental distress.

The procedure itself was as unsettling as its purpose. Patients were forcibly placed in the Tranquilizer Chair, with their limbs and sometimes their heads secured in restraints. The chair's design often included a high back and armrests to make it difficult for the patient to move or escape. The immobility and restraint could last for hours or even days.

The rationale behind the Tranquilizer Chair was fundamentally flawed, rooted in a lack of understanding of the complexities of mental illness. Mental disorders are multifaceted, with causes that can be biological, psychological, and social in nature. Attempting to "calm" individuals by forcibly immobilizing them ignored the underlying causes of their distress and exacerbated the already significant challenges they faced.

In many cases, the use of the Tranquilizer Chair led to physical and psychological harm. Patients often experienced extreme discomfort, muscle stiffness, and a sense of helplessness. Prolonged immobilization could lead to physical complications, including pressure sores, muscle atrophy, and deep vein thrombosis. The psychological toll of being forcibly restrained and immobilized was profound, adding to the distress of individuals already grappling with mental illness.

The practice of using the Tranquilizer Chair was not limited to any particular region or time period. It was employed in psychiatric hospitals and asylums throughout the 19th and early 20th centuries, and it persisted even as the field of psychiatry evolved. The enduring use of the Tranquilizer Chair underscores the deep-seated misunderstanding of mental illness and the desperation to find solutions in the absence of effective treatments.

During the late 19th and early 20th centuries, the field of psychiatry was marked by a shift toward more humane and compassionate approaches to mental health care. The introduction of psychotherapy, along with the development of psychoactive medications, marked a turning point in the treatment of mental disorders. These advancements emphasized the importance of understanding and addressing the underlying causes of mental illness rather than simply restraining or immobilizing patients.

Despite these advances, the use of the Tranquilizer Chair persisted in some psychiatric institutions well into the 20th century. Its continued use was often driven by a combination of habit, a lack of awareness of alternative approaches. In some cases, it was driven by a disregard for the rights and dignity of individuals with mental illnesses.

The history of the Tranquilizer Chair is a stark reminder of the ethical and human rights challenges that have characterized the treatment of individuals with mental disorders. The practice of forcibly immobilizing patients in this manner raises profound ethical questions about the treatment of vulnerable individuals.

In the mid-20th century, as the understanding of mental illness continued to evolve, the use of the Tranquilizer Chair began to wane. It was increasingly recognized as an outdated and inhumane practice, and ethical concerns surrounding its use gained prominence. The need to uphold the rights and dignity of individuals with mental illnesses became a central tenet of modern mental health care.

The story of the Tranquilizer Chair serves as a haunting reminder of the darkness that once shrouded the field of mental health care. It highlights the importance of continuously reassessing and improving our understanding of mental illness, as well as our commitment to compassionate, evidence-based, and ethical approaches to treatment.

The experiences of those who endured the use of the Tranquilizer Chair are a testament to the resilience of individuals living with mental illness. They also signify the ethical responsibility of the medical community to provide care that is respectful, compassionate, and effective. This story underscores the imperative of never compromising the rights and dignity of individuals, regardless of the challenges they face.

As we reflect on the history of the Tranquilizer Chair, we are reminded of the progress that has been made in the field of mental health care. It serves as a powerful illustration of the necessity of ongoing advancement and the unwavering commitment to providing the most humane and effective treatments for mental disorders. In the journey towards understanding, empathy, and ethical responsibility, the dark history of the Tranquilizer Chair stands as a somber milestone on the path to more compassionate and effective mental health care.

6. Blistering

Blistering involved intentionally creating blisters on a patient's skin by applying irritating substances. This was done in the belief that it would draw out "excess" or "bad" humors, which were thought to be the cause of mental illness. The history of blistering is a chilling testament to the desperate quest for solutions and the human suffering it often caused.

The practice of blistering as a treatment for mental illness has its origins in ancient medical traditions and beliefs. It was rooted in the theory of humorism, which posited that the balance of bodily fluids, or "humors" (blood, phlegm, black bile, and yellow bile), determined an individual's health and temperament. An imbalance in these humors was thought to lead to physical and mental ailments. In the context of mental health treatment, blistering was based on the idea that the mental illness was caused by an excess of "bad" humors within the body. The creation of blisters on the skin was believed to draw out and eliminate these supposed impurities, thereby restoring the balance of humors and, in turn, curing the mental illness.

The procedure itself was as gruesome as its intent. Patients subjected to blistering would have irritating substances applied to their skin, commonly cantharidin, a toxic compound derived from the blister beetle. Cantharidin caused severe skin irritation and blister formation, often accompanied by intense pain and inflammation. The process was as painful as it was distressing, and patients frequently endured agony as they watched their skin blister and fester.

The restraints employed to hold patients down during the blistering process added to the horror of the treatment. Leather straps and physical force were often used to ensure the patient's compliance and immobility during this painful procedure. The patient's cries and pleas for mercy would frequently fall on deaf ears, as physicians believed that this excruciating treatment was a necessary means of restoring their mental health.

The procedure was not only physically distressing but also carried significant risks. Blisters created through blistering could become infected, leading to severe complications. Prolonged pain, scarring, and disfigurement often resulted from this practice, which was undertaken with the hope of relieving mental distress. Far from providing relief, blistering was more likely to exacerbate the suffering of patients struggling with mental illness.

Despite the dubious scientific basis and the physical and psychological suffering it caused, blistering persisted as a treatment for mental illness for centuries. During the 18th and 19th centuries, mental health care was marked by a limited understanding of mental illness.

Consequently, patients who exhibited symptoms of mental disorders, such as agitation, depression, or hallucinations, were often subjected to blistering in a misguided attempt to alleviate their suffering.

The use of blistering was not confined to a particular geographic region but appeared as a widespread and enduring practice. It was employed in psychiatric hospitals, asylums, and by various medical practitioners who believed in the theories of humorism. The enduring use of blistering underscores the deep-seated misunderstanding of mental illness and the desperation to find solutions in the absence of effective treatments.

During the late 19th and early 20th centuries, the field of psychiatry began to shift towards more humane and compassionate approaches to mental health care. As a result, blistering began to fall out of favor. Emerging scientific theories and the development of psychoactive medications marked a significant turning point in the treatment of mental disorders. These innovations emphasized the importance of understanding and addressing the underlying causes of mental illness, rather than resorting to painful and scientifically unfounded treatments.

While blistering as a mental health treatment has largely been abandoned, its historical use remains a chilling reminder of the challenges and ethical dilemmas that have marked the treatment of individuals with mental disorders. The practice of creating blisters on a patient's skin raises profound ethical questions about the treatment of vulnerable individuals. It also highlights the responsibility of the medical community to provide care that is respectful, compassionate, and effective.

As we reflect on the history of blistering, we are reminded of the progress that has been made in the field of mental health care. The story of blistering is a powerful illustration of the necessity of ongoing advancement, as well as the unwavering commitment to providing the most humane and effective treatments for mental disorders. It underscores the imperative of never compromising the rights and dignity of individuals, regardless of the challenges they face.

The experiences of those who endured the use of blistering are a testament to the resilience of individuals living with mental illness. They also represent the ethical responsibility of the medical community to provide care that is respectful, compassionate, and effective. It is through understanding, empathy, and ethical responsibility that we can continue to advance the field of mental health care. We should ensure the well-being and dignity of all individuals living with mental disorders.

7. Cold Water Bathing

Cold water bathing involved subjecting patients to cold water baths, and at times even ice baths, with the belief that such shock therapy would alleviate mental disorders. The history of cold water bathing is a chilling testament to the misguided efforts to treat mental illness, marked by a severe lack of scientific understanding.

The practice of cold water bathing as a treatment for mental disorders can be traced back to the late 18th and early 19th centuries. During this period, the prevailing theories about mental illnesses were heavily influenced by the belief in the connection between the mind and the body. It was thought that the root causes of mental disorders could be found in the physical constitution, and therefore, treatments often focused on altering the body to affect the mind.

The rationale behind cold water bathing was rooted in the belief that the mind and body were intrinsically linked, and that manipulating the body through extreme physical measures could influence the state of the mind. It was posited that by subjecting patients to the shock of cold water, their mental agitation and disturbances could be disrupted and ultimately alleviated. The procedure itself was as distressing as its intent. Patients would be forcibly immersed in cold water, often as part of a regimen that included repeated baths over extended periods. In some cases, ice baths were used, intensifying the cold and discomfort. Patients' reactions to the cold water varied, but many experienced extreme shock, discomfort, and panic.

The proponents of cold water bathing believed that the shock caused by the cold water would have a "resetting" effect on the mind. They thought it would interrupt the thought patterns associated with mental disorders and induce a state of calm. This belief was rooted in the misguided notion that mental disorders were a result of abnormalities in brain function that could be disrupted and corrected through external intervention.

The chilling effects of cold water bathing were not only physical but also psychological. Patients often described feeling a profound sense of fear, confusion, and distress during and after the treatment. The procedure's discomfort, combined with the already challenging experience of mental illness, added to the suffering of those subjected to cold water baths.

Moreover, the ethical concerns surrounding cold water bathing were substantial. Patients were often subjected to this treatment without their informed consent, a fundamental violation of their rights. The practice was also physically risky, as prolonged exposure to cold water could lead to hypothermia, frostbite, and other medical complications. In some cases, it resulted in severe injuries or even death.

Despite these concerns and the often questionable efficacy of the treatment, cold water bathing was widely used in mental health institutions and asylums during the 19th century. The practice persisted, driven by the desperation of medical professionals and families to find a solution for individuals suffering from mental disorders. The continued use of cold water bathing was not limited to a particular region or time period. It was employed across Europe and North America, reflecting a shared belief in the potential benefits of the treatment. While some physicians were skeptical of its effectiveness, others were convinced that the cold water's shock therapy could indeed alleviate mental distress.

The historical use of cold water bathing underscores the limitations of mental health care during the 19th century and the ethical dilemmas that marked the treatment of individuals with mental disorders. It highlights the imperative of advancing scientific understanding and prioritizing the well-being and dignity of patients in mental health care. In the mid-20th century, as the field of psychiatry continued to evolve, the use of cold water bathing began to wane. Emerging scientific theories, including advancements in psychotherapy and the development of psychoactive medications, marked a significant turning point in the treatment of mental disorders. These innovations emphasized the importance of understanding and addressing the underlying causes of mental illness, rather than resorting to painful and scientifically unfounded treatments.

While cold water bathing for mental health treatment has largely been abandoned, its historical use remains a chilling reminder of the challenges and ethical dilemmas that have characterized the treatment of individuals with mental disorders. The practice of subjecting patients to extreme cold water therapy raises profound ethical questions about the treatment of vulnerable individuals and the responsibility of the medical community to provide care that is respectful, compassionate, and effective.

As we reflect on the history of cold water bathing, we are reminded of the progress that has been made in the field of mental health care. The story of this chilling treatment is a powerful illustration of the necessity of ongoing advancement and the unwavering commitment to providing the most humane and effective treatments for mental disorders. It underscores the imperative of never compromising the rights and dignity of individuals, regardless of the challenges they face.

The experiences of those who endured cold water bathing indicate the resilience of individuals living with mental illness. It shows the ethical responsibility of the medical community to provide care that is respectful, compassionate, and effective. It is through understanding, empathy, and ethical responsibility that we can continue to advance the field of mental health care. We should ensure the well-being and dignity of all individuals living with mental disorders.

8. Iron Masks and Restraints

The use of iron masks and restraints as a means of controlling behavior in individuals with mental disorders is a haunting chapter in the history of mental health care. These brutal interventions, driven by a fundamental misunderstanding of mental illness and the desire to manage individuals deemed "mad," are a stark reminder of the dark and inhumane practices that have marked the field of psychiatry.

Iron masks and restraints, designed to confine and immobilize patients, were particularly prevalent during the late 18th and 19th centuries. During this period, mental health care was characterized by limited understanding of mental disorders, and the prevailing theories often attributed such conditions to moral or character flaws. In the absence of effective treatments, the management of individuals with mental illnesses often turned to extreme and inhumane methods.

The practice of using iron masks and restraints was rooted in the belief that individuals with mental disorders needed to be physically controlled and confined to prevent them from causing harm to themselves or others. It was often seen as the only means of managing those considered "unmanageable" due to their mental conditions.

The concept of the iron mask was particularly gruesome. Patients would be fitted with a heavy, metal mask that covered their entire face, including their eyes, nose, and mouth. This effectively deprived them of their sensory perceptions and made breathing and speaking difficult. The iron mask was designed to restrict movement and prevent the patient from biting or attacking others.

Restraints, including straitjackets and shackles, were also commonly used to confine individuals with mental disorders. These restraints would limit the patient's ability to move their arms, legs, or even their entire body. Patients were often tied to their beds or confined to small, restrictive spaces for extended periods.

The physical and psychological toll of these interventions was profound. Patients subjected to iron masks and restraints experienced extreme discomfort, pain, and distress. The iron mask, in particular, was a source of intense suffering, as it deprived individuals of their sensory experiences, causing disorientation and anxiety. The inability to speak or communicate further isolated patients, intensifying their feelings of helplessness.

The ethical concerns surrounding the use of iron masks and restraints were significant. Patients were often subjected to these treatments without their informed consent, and the practices were carried out in a manner that violated the individual's rights and dignity. The physical and psychological suffering they endured was inhumane, as it often far exceeded the distress caused by their underlying mental disorders.

The historical use of iron masks and restraints is a harrowing reminder of the challenges and ethical dilemmas that have marked the treatment of individuals with mental disorders. It underscores the importance of advancing scientific understanding and prioritizing the well-being and dignity of patients in mental health care.

During the late 19th and early 20th centuries, the field of psychiatry began to shift towards more humane and compassionate approaches to mental health care. Emerging scientific theories and the development of psychotherapy marked a significant turning point in the treatment of mental disorders. These innovations emphasized the importance of understanding and addressing the underlying causes of mental illness, rather than resorting to painful and scientifically unfounded treatments. The use of iron masks and restraints in mental health care began to decline as these more humane and evidence-based practices gained prominence. Ethical concerns and public outrage contributed to the abandonment of these cruel interventions.

The historical use of iron masks and restraints may be a chilling testament to the treatment of individuals with mental disorders. It also serves as a reminder of the progress that has been made in the field of mental health care. The story of these brutal interventions highlights the imperative of continually advancing scientific understanding, ethical responsibility, and compassionate care for individuals living with mental disorders.

The experiences of those who endured the use of iron masks and restraints are a testament to the resilience of individuals living with mental illness and the responsibility of the medical community to provide care that is respectful, compassionate, and effective. It is through understanding, empathy, and ethical responsibility that we can continue to advance the field of mental health care. This helps us ensure the well-being and dignity of all individuals living with mental disorders.

9. Phrenology

In the annals of medical history, few practices have been as bizarre and now discredited as phrenology. The once-popular belief that the shape and contours of the skull could reveal personality traits and the propensity for mental health conditions, phrenology was touted as a groundbreaking science in the 19th century. However, it is now recognized as a pseudoscience, a testament to the limitations of medical knowledge and the dangers of drawing sweeping conclusions about mental health based on superficial observations.

Phrenology gained prominence in the late 18th and early 19th centuries. It was founded on the notion that the brain was the seat of human personality and that the shape and size of specific brain regions, reflected in the contours of the skull, could provide insights into an individual's character and mental abilities.

Franz Joseph Gall, a German physician, is often credited as the father of phrenology. He believed that the human brain was divided into multiple distinct organs, each responsible for a specific mental function. Gall hypothesized that the size and development of these brain organs could be assessed by examining the bumps, depressions, and contours on the skull's surface. He argued that a person's personality, intelligence, and tendencies could be determined by examining these cranial features.

Phrenologists, as practitioners of this pseudoscience came to be known, claimed that by measuring the dimensions and characteristics of the skull, they could gain insight into an individual's predisposition to various mental health conditions. For example, they asserted that an enlarged region of the skull might indicate a propensity for criminal behavior, while a differently shaped area might signify artistic talent or benevolence.

Phrenology quickly gained popularity, captivating the public's imagination and sparking debates among scientists, physicians, and laypeople. It was touted as a means of unlocking the mysteries of the human mind and predicting future behaviors based on cranial examinations. The practice promised to provide a new understanding of mental health and the ability to identify potential issues early.

Despite its initial appeal, phrenology was deeply flawed and had numerous problems that undermined its legitimacy as a science. Phrenology was based on anecdotal observations rather than rigorous scientific evidence. The measurements and assessments of the skull were highly subjective and prone to bias. Additionally, Phrenologists' division of the brain into discrete "organs" responsible for specific traits oversimplified the complexity of brain function. In reality, the brain is a highly interconnected organ, and the relationship between its various regions is far more intricate.

Also, phrenologists made grandiose claims about the ability to predict future behavior, diagnose mental health conditions, and even identify criminal tendencies based on skull measurements. These assertions lacked empirical support and were often sensationalized.This intervention was also riddled with racial and gender biases. Phrenologists used their pseudoscience to justify harmful stereotypes and reinforce prejudices.

The practice of phrenology raised ethical concerns, particularly when used to assess an individual's character or fitness for employment. Employers and authorities would sometimes rely on phrenological examinations to make important decisions.

The influence of phrenology on mental health understanding was, at best, misguided and, at worst, harmful. Phrenologists attempted to associate the shapes of cranial features with various mental health conditions. For example, they claimed that individuals with specific head shapes were more prone to conditions like depression, anxiety, or even psychosis.

In practice, the pseudoscience of phrenology often resulted in misdiagnoses and inappropriate treatments. Individuals deemed to have "abnormal" skull shapes were sometimes subjected to therapies that were painful or degrading. The stigmatization of those with distinctive cranial features added an additional layer of suffering to individuals already grappling with mental health challenges.

Moreover, phrenology contributed to the harmful notion that mental health conditions could be reduced to simple physical attributes. This idea detracted from the emerging understanding of mental health as a complex interplay of biological, psychological, and social factors. The oversimplified approach of phrenology hindered the development of more accurate and empathetic ways of understanding and addressing mental health.

Over time, the flaws and controversies surrounding phrenology began to erode its credibility. Skepticism among the scientific community grew, and the limitations of the practice became more apparent. By the mid-19th century, phrenology was largely discredited as a legitimate science, though it continued to have a presence in popular culture for some time.

The story of phrenology is a stark reminder of the dangers of pseudoscientific practices and the harm they can inflict on individuals, particularly those with mental health challenges. Phrenology, despite its fallacious foundation, had real-world consequences for many people, reinforcing stereotypes and contributing to the stigmatization of mental illness.

The legacy of phrenology is a cautionary tale, highlighting the importance of rigorous scientific inquiry and ethical considerations in the field of mental health care. It underscores the need for evidence-based practices, empathy, and an understanding that mental health is a complex and multifaceted aspect of human well-being.

Today, the field of mental health care has advanced significantly, with a deeper understanding of the biological, psychological, and social factors that contribute to mental health conditions. Treatments are based on empirical evidence, ethical principles, and a commitment to the well-being and dignity of individuals living with mental disorders. Phrenology, once a widely accepted practice, now stands as a stark reminder of the importance of skepticism, scientific rigor, and compassion in the pursuit of effective mental health care.

10. Psychosurgery

In the annals of medical history, there are practices that, despite their intentions, resulted in unimaginable suffering for countless individuals. One such practice, now regarded as a dark chapter in the field of mental health care, is psychosurgery. Early forms of psychosurgery, most notably the infamous lobotomies, involved physically altering the brain in an attempt to treat mental illness. These procedures, conducted with the hope of alleviating the suffering of individuals with severe psychiatric conditions, often led to severe side effects and are no longer practiced. The story of psychosurgery is a harrowing tale of medical experimentation, ethical dilemmas, and the enduring commitment to finding humane and effective treatments for mental illness.

Psychosurgery, as a medical intervention for mental illness, gained attention in the early 20th century. Its origins can be traced to the work of Portuguese neurologist Egas Moniz and his development of a procedure known as prefrontal leucotomy, which was later popularized and modified by American neurologist Walter Freeman.

The rationale behind psychosurgery was rooted in the belief that by physically altering specific areas of the brain, it was possible to alleviate the symptoms of severe mental illness. It was thought that by disconnecting or removing neural pathways, the troublesome symptoms associated with conditions like schizophrenia, severe depression, and anxiety disorders could be reduced or eliminated.

Lobotomies, the most well-known form of psychosurgery, involved the insertion of a surgical instrument, such as an orbitoclast or leucotome, through the eye sockets or the skull to damage the frontal lobes of the brain. The frontal lobes play a crucial role in regulating mood, personality, and decision-making. By damaging these regions, it was believed that patients would become more manageable and their symptoms would be alleviated.

The early years of lobotomies were marked by enthusiastic experimentation, as well as by the hope that these procedures could offer relief to individuals who had been deemed "incurable." However, the tragic consequences of lobotomies soon became evident.

Patients who underwent lobotomies often experienced severe side effects, including changes in personality, emotional blunting, cognitive impairment, and a loss of motivation. While some individuals did show a reduction in the intensity of their symptoms, these improvements came at an enormous cost. Many patients emerged from lobotomies as shadows of their former selves, stripped of their vitality and humanity.

The procedure was often performed on vulnerable populations, including institutionalized individuals, and it was sometimes carried out without informed consent. Patients were frequently subjected to lobotomies against their will or the will of their families. This unethical practice raised profound questions about medical ethics and the rights of individuals with mental illness. The widespread use of lobotomies and other forms of psychosurgery gave rise to significant ethical dilemmas. While some physicians and advocates argued that these procedures offered a last resort for individuals who had not responded to other treatments, others raised concerns about the ethical implications of permanently altering a person's brain.

The medical community began to grapple with the moral questions surrounding psychosurgery, as well as the need for more rigorous scientific evaluation of its efficacy and safety. Informed consent became a central issue, and there was a growing recognition of the importance of upholding the rights and dignity of individuals with mental illness.

The widespread use of lobotomies and psychosurgery began to wane in the mid-20th century. The limitations and ethical concerns surrounding these procedures became increasingly evident. The introduction of antipsychotic medications, psychotherapy, and other forms of psychiatric treatment offered more effective and humane alternatives. The advent of medications such as chlorpromazine revolutionized the treatment of mental illness. They provided relief for many individuals with conditions like schizophrenia and bipolar disorder without the need for invasive and risky surgical procedures.

Additionally, the efforts of mental health advocates and organizations helped raise awareness of the ethical concerns surrounding psychosurgery. This led to changes in medical practice and greater attention to informed consent, patient rights, and the importance of considering less invasive treatment options.

The legacy of psychosurgery is a sobering reminder of the challenges and ethical dilemmas that have marked the treatment of individuals with mental disorders. It underscores the importance of evidence-based and ethical practices in the field of mental health care. Psychosurgery is no longer practiced in the form of lobotomies or other similarly invasive procedures. However, the history of these interventions is a reminder of the enduring commitment to finding humane and effective treatments for mental illness. It also highlights the necessity of upholding the rights and dignity of individuals with mental disorders, particularly in moments of vulnerability.

The experiences of those who underwent lobotomies are a testament to the resilience of individuals living with mental illness. They also remind us of the ethical responsibility of the medical community to provide care that is respectful, compassionate, and effective. Today, the field of mental health care has come a long way, emphasizing evidence-based treatments, ethical principles, and the importance of informed consent. The rights of individuals with mental disorders are enshrined in various legal and ethical frameworks, with a focus on ensuring their dignity and autonomy.

The story of psychosurgery, particularly the tragic history of lobotomies, serves as a haunting reminder of the darkness that once shrouded the field of mental health care. It underscores the imperative of never compromising the rights and dignity of individuals, regardless of the challenges they face. It also highlights the ongoing commitment to providing the most humane and effective treatments for mental disorders.

11.   Spinal Osteopathy

Spinal osteopathy held the unfounded belief that manipulating the spine could alleviate a wide range of conditions, including mental health disorders. Despite its proponents' claims, spinal osteopathy was built on shaky scientific ground and has since been largely discredited. The story of spinal osteopathy is a striking illustration of the challenges and pitfalls in the pursuit of effective treatments for mental health conditions.

The practice of spinal osteopathy emerged in the late 19th and early 20th centuries. This was a time when medical knowledge and understanding of the human body were still in their infancy. Osteopathy itself was founded by Dr. Andrew Taylor Still, who believed in the importance of the musculoskeletal system in maintaining overall health. Osteopathy, as a discipline, focused on the concept that the body's structure and function were closely interconnected. Practitioners of osteopathy argued that by manipulating the musculoskeletal system, various ailments, including those related to mental health, could be alleviated.

One offshoot of osteopathy was spinal osteopathy, which placed a particular emphasis on the spine as a key to well-being. It was believed that the spine housed a complex network of nerves. Consequently, manipulating the vertebrae and the surrounding structures, practitioners could influence the nervous system and, consequently, various physical and mental conditions. It was posited that disorders such as anxiety, depression, and even psychosis could be treated by realigning the spine. These claims were made with little scientific validation or empirical evidence.

Spinal osteopathy practitioners often described the human body in metaphysical terms. They spoke of a vital force that flowed through the spine and the necessity of maintaining its uninterrupted flow. The focus on this vital force and the belief that spinal manipulation could unblock it was central to the practice. While some patients reported experiencing temporary relief from symptoms after spinal osteopathy treatments, the lack of scientific rigor in the practice raised numerous concerns. The treatment's effectiveness often relied on anecdotal evidence and the placebo effect rather than rigorous scientific study.

Moreover, the use of spinal osteopathy to address mental health disorders raised ethical questions. Patients, often grappling with serious mental health conditions, were drawn to this unconventional approach out of desperation for relief. The lack of scientific validation and the potential for financial exploitation of vulnerable individuals were pressing concerns. Over time, the limitations and questionable scientific basis of spinal osteopathy became increasingly evident. Skepticism among the medical and scientific communities grew, and the need for empirical evidence to support the practice became undeniable. The field of mental health also evolved, with a growing emphasis on evidence-based treatments, psychotherapy, and pharmacotherapy. As this shift occurred, spinal osteopathy and similar alternative treatments for mental health became increasingly marginalized.

The legacy of spinal osteopathy serves as a reminder of the importance of rigorous scientific inquiry and evidence-based practices in the field of mental health care. It underscores the dangers of unsubstantiated claims and the exploitation of individuals seeking relief from mental health conditions. Today, the field of mental health care has advanced significantly, with a deeper understanding of the biological, psychological, and social factors that contribute to mental health conditions. Treatments are based on empirical evidence, ethical principles, and a commitment to the well-being and dignity of individuals living with mental disorders.

While spinal osteopathy and similar practices have largely been abandoned, their historical use remains a cautionary tale. The story of spinal osteopathy highlights the need for a compassionate and evidence-based approach to mental health care. It also reflects the responsibility of the medical community to provide care that is respectful, effective, and informed by scientific research.

The experiences of those who sought relief through spinal osteopathy are a testament to the complexity of mental health conditions and the vulnerability of individuals living with these disorders. It is through understanding, empathy, and ethical responsibility that we can continue to advance the field of mental health care and ensure the well-being and dignity of all individuals living with mental disorders.

12. Blood Transfusions

Blood transfusion was an early 20th century belief that blood transfusions from "healthy" individuals to those with mental illness could cure a wide array of psychiatric disorders. Despite the earnest intentions of some practitioners, this practice had no scientific basis and is now recognized as a bizarre and ineffective approach to treating mental health conditions. The story of blood transfusions in mental health care is a testament to the quest for innovative solutions, even in the absence of concrete evidence.

At the dawn of the 20th century, the field of medicine was a landscape of burgeoning discoveries and novel therapies. Blood transfusions, which had been established as a life-saving technique for treating various medical conditions, were seen as revolutionary. They offered hope for individuals suffering from a multitude of illnesses, including those with psychiatric disorders.

Some practitioners, influenced by the general enthusiasm surrounding blood transfusions, began to explore the potential benefits of this procedure for individuals with mental health conditions. It was posited that by infusing the blood of "healthy" individuals into those grappling with mental illnesses, a transformative and curative effect could be achieved. This belief was built on an optimistic view of the power of blood to influence the body and mind.

The central issue with the use of blood transfusions to treat mental illness was the lack of scientific validation. The practice was based on a flawed premise: that mental health disorders were directly connected to the quality or characteristics of a person's blood. This notion disregarded the complex and multifaceted nature of mental health and the myriad factors that contribute to these conditions.

Furthermore, the practice of transferring blood from one individual to another, known as heterologous blood transfusion, carried inherent risks. It often resulted in serious complications, such as blood type incompatibility, transfusion reactions, and the transmission of infectious diseases. These adverse outcomes were particularly problematic for vulnerable individuals with mental health conditions.

The use of blood transfusions to treat mental illness raised profound ethical concerns. Many patients subjected to this treatment were vulnerable and in desperate need of relief from their psychiatric symptoms. Their conditions often left them feeling isolated, stigmatized, and without effective treatments. In some cases, patients received blood transfusions without their informed consent or under duress. The financial exploitation of individuals seeking relief from their mental health conditions was also a pressing concern. This exploitation was driven by the belief that individuals with mental illness were willing to pay exorbitant sums for a cure, even if the treatment itself had no scientific basis.

Over time, the limitations and ethical concerns surrounding blood transfusions in the treatment of mental illness became increasingly evident. The scientific community began to question the validity of this approach, and skepticism grew. The field of mental health care also advanced, with a growing emphasis on evidence-based treatments, psychotherapy, and pharmacotherapy. As this shift occurred, the use of blood transfusions in mental health care gradually waned.

The legacy of blood transfusions in mental health care is a stark reminder of the dangers of unsubstantiated claims and the exploitation of individuals seeking relief from mental health conditions. It underscores the need for evidence-based and ethical practices in the field of mental health care.

The use of blood transfusions in the treatment of mental illness may seem like a bizarre and misguided practice in retrospect. However, it is a testament to the complexity of mental health conditions and the vulnerability of individuals living with these disorders. It is through understanding, empathy, and ethical responsibility that we can continue to advance the field of mental health care and ensure the well-being and dignity of all individuals living with mental disorders.

The story of blood transfusions in mental health care, and the enduring commitment to finding innovative solutions, is a reminder of the importance of rigorous scientific inquiry and ethical considerations in the field of mental health care. It underscores the imperative of never compromising the rights and dignity of individuals, regardless of the challenges they face. It also highlights the ongoing commitment to providing the most humane and effective treatments for mental disorders.

13. Insulin-Induced Comas

Insulin-induced comas was employed in an effort to treat conditions like schizophrenia. Although it offered a glimmer of hope, this procedure had grave consequences, and its use has long been discontinued. The story of insulin-induced comas in the context of mental health care serves as a poignant illustration of the complex journey towards finding humane and effective treatments for psychiatric conditions.

The use of insulin-induced comas for the treatment of mental health disorders found its roots in the early 20th century. The treatment was based on the theory that certain mental illnesses, such as schizophrenia, were linked to abnormal metabolic processes in the brain. It was believed that by inducing a state of hypoglycemia (low blood sugar) through insulin injections, the metabolic abnormalities associated with mental illness could be corrected, offering a potential cure.

The procedure involved administering high doses of insulin to patients, leading to a rapid drop in blood sugar levels. As blood glucose levels plummeted, the patient would slip into a coma-like state, which would typically last for about an hour. The coma was induced multiple times a week, and patients would often receive several treatments over the course of several months.

Insulin-induced comas provided a sense of hope to individuals with mental health disorders and their families. At the time, the field of psychiatry was in its infancy, and effective treatments for conditions like schizophrenia were limited. The idea of a medical procedure that could potentially alleviate the tormenting symptoms of mental illness was met with optimism.

However, this optimism was tempered by the significant risks associated with insulin-induced comas. The procedure carried numerous dangers, including the potential for severe hypoglycemia, convulsions, and even death. Patients undergoing insulin-induced comas were subjected to substantial physical and psychological stress, and the risks often outweighed any potential benefits.

Over time, the limitations and risks of insulin-induced comas became increasingly apparent. The scientific community began to question the validity of this approach, and skepticism grew. The advent of antipsychotic medications marked a significant turning point in the treatment of mental health disorders. These medications provided effective relief for individuals with conditions like schizophrenia without the need for risky and invasive procedures.

Furthermore, ethical concerns about the use of insulin-induced comas began to gain prominence. Questions were raised about the necessity of informed consent, the rights of patients, and the ethical responsibility of the medical community. The severe risks and questionable effectiveness of the procedure weighed heavily on its continued use.

As a result, the use of insulin-induced comas in the treatment of mental health disorders was gradually phased out. More humane and effective approaches to psychiatric treatment, including psychotherapy and medication, came to the forefront.

The legacy of insulin-induced comas in the context of mental health care is a sobering reminder of the challenges and ethical dilemmas that have marked the treatment of individuals with psychiatric conditions. It underscores the importance of evidence-based and ethical practices in the field of mental health care. The experiences of those who underwent insulin-induced comas are a testament to the complexity of mental health conditions and the vulnerability of individuals living with these disorders.

Today, the field of mental health care has come a long way, emphasizing evidence-based treatments, ethical principles, and the importance of informed consent and patient rights. The story of insulin-induced comas may seem like a perplexing and misguided chapter in the history of psychiatric treatment. However, it serves as a stark reminder of the need for a compassionate and evidence-based approach to mental health care.

14. Mesmerism

The pages of medical history are replete with tales of unconventional and, at times, bewildering treatments for a multitude of ailments. One such practice, known as mesmerism or animal magnetism, sought to employ magnets and hypnosis to treat a variety of conditions, including mental health disorders. Despite its proponents' fervent beliefs, mesmerism is now widely regarded as pseudoscience—a curious chapter in the ongoing quest to understand and address mental health conditions. The story of mesmerism in mental health care serves as an illuminating example of the evolving perceptions of therapeutic interventions and the unending quest for innovative solutions.

The practice of mesmerism found its roots in the late 18th century with Franz Anton Mesmer, a German physician. Mesmer believed in the existence of a universal life force, which he referred to as "animal magnetism." He postulated that imbalances in this life force led to various physical and mental ailments. Mesmerism revolved around the idea that individuals could harness this life force and use it to bring about healing. Practitioners of mesmerism believed that through the use of magnets or the power of suggestion, they could restore harmony to the patient's life force, thereby curing their ailments.

Mesmerism was closely associated with the practice of hypnosis. The mesmerist, often using elaborate rituals and dramatic hand gestures, would place patients into a trance-like state through deep concentration and focused attention. In this altered state, it was believed that the patient's subconscious mind could be accessed and manipulated to address various conditions, including those related to mental health.

Magnets were another integral aspect of mesmerism. Magnets, both permanent and artificial, were applied to the patient's body to supposedly realign the life force and alleviate physical and mental maladies. It was believed that the magnetic fields could influence the patient's nervous system and brain, leading to improved mental health.

Mesmerism gained popularity in the late 18th and early 19th centuries, with practitioners making grandiose claims about its effectiveness in treating a wide range of ailments, including mental health disorders. It was touted as a revolutionary approach to healing, particularly in a time when medical knowledge was limited. However, the claims of mesmerists were often unsubstantiated, and the practice was marked by a lack of scientific rigor. The concept of "animal magnetism" and its supposed influence on mental health was built on subjective experiences and anecdotal evidence.

The ethical questions surrounding mesmerism were also profound. Patients undergoing hypnotic trances were often highly suggestible and vulnerable to manipulation. The potential for exploitation and harm, particularly in the realm of mental health, raised serious ethical concerns. Over time, the limitations and ethical concerns surrounding mesmerism became increasingly evident. The scientific community began to question the validity of this approach, and skepticism grew.

The field of mental health care advanced with the emergence of more evidence-based practices, including psychotherapy and, eventually, psychopharmacology. As these approaches gained prominence, the use of mesmerism in mental health care gradually waned. The legacy of mesmerism in mental health care serves as a stark reminder of the dangers of pseudoscientific practices and the potential for exploitation of individuals seeking relief from mental health conditions. It underscores the need for evidence-based and ethical practices in the field of mental health care.

Today, the field of mental health care has made significant progress, emphasizing evidence-based treatments, ethical principles, and the importance of informed consent and patient rights. The story of mesmerism may appear as an eccentric and fanciful episode in the history of mental health care. It serves as a valuable reminder of the imperative for a compassionate and evidence-based approach to mental health care.

The experiences of those who sought relief through mesmerism are a testament to the complexity of mental health conditions and the vulnerability of individuals living with these disorders. We should continue to advance the field of mental health care and ensure the well-being and dignity of all individuals living with mental disorders.

15.   Frontal Lobotomy

Frontal lobotomy is a chilling testament to the lengths to which medical practitioners once went in their quest to treat mental illness. This surgical procedure involved removing or damaging the frontal lobes of the brain and was widely employed in the mid-20th century but is now deemed highly unethical and dangerous. The story of frontal lobotomy is a harrowing tale of medical experimentation, ethical quandaries, and the enduring search for humane and effective treatments for mental illness.

Frontal lobotomy had its roots in the work of Portuguese neurologist Egas Moniz. Moniz developed a technique known as prefrontal leucotomy in the 1930s. The procedure was later modified and popularized by American neurologist Walter Freeman, earning it the name "lobotomy." The central premise behind frontal lobotomies was the belief that by altering the frontal lobes, it was possible to ameliorate the symptoms of severe mental illness. The frontal lobes are critical in regulating emotions, decision-making, and personality. By damaging these areas, it was thought that patients with psychiatric conditions would become more manageable and their symptoms would be reduced.

The early years of lobotomies were marked by enthusiastic experimentation, and the hope that this procedure could provide relief for individuals who had been considered "incurable." Yet the tragic consequences of frontal lobotomies quickly became evident. Patients who underwent lobotomies often experienced severe side effects, including changes in personality, emotional blunting, cognitive impairment, and a loss of motivation. While some individuals did show a reduction in the intensity of their symptoms, these improvements came at an enormous cost. Many patients emerged from lobotomies as mere shadows of their former selves, stripped of their vitality and humanity.

The procedure was often performed on vulnerable populations, particularly those institutionalized in mental asylums, and in some cases, it was done without informed consent. Patients were frequently subjected to lobotomies against their will or the will of their families.

This unethical practice raised profound questions about medical ethics and the rights of individuals with mental illness. Some physicians and advocates argued that these procedures offered a last resort for individuals who had not responded to other treatments. Others raised concerns about the ethical implications of permanently altering a person's brain.

The medical community began to grapple with the moral questions surrounding lobotomies, as well as the need for more rigorous scientific evaluation of its efficacy and safety. Informed consent became a central issue, and there was a growing recognition of the importance of upholding the rights and dignity of individuals with mental illness.

The widespread use of frontal lobotomies began to wane in the mid-20th century as the limitations and ethical concerns surrounding these procedures became increasingly evident. The introduction of antipsychotic medications, psychotherapy, and other forms of psychiatric treatment offered more effective and humane alternatives. Medications such as chlorpromazine revolutionized the treatment of mental illness, providing relief for many individuals with conditions like schizophrenia and bipolar disorder without the need for invasive and risky surgical procedures.

Additionally, the efforts of mental health advocates and organizations helped raise awareness of the ethical concerns surrounding lobotomies. This led to changes in medical practice and greater attention to informed consent, patient rights, and the importance of considering less invasive treatment options. The legacy of frontal lobotomies is a haunting reminder of the darkness that once shrouded the field of mental health care. It underscores the importance of evidence-based and ethical practices in the field of mental health care.

Frontal lobotomies are no longer practiced in their original form.However, the history of these interventions serves as a reminder of the enduring commitment to finding humane and effective treatments for mental illness. It also highlights the necessity of upholding the rights and dignity of individuals with mental disorders, particularly in moments of vulnerability.

The story of frontal lobotomies, particularly the tragic history of these procedures, serves as a cautionary tale. It underscores the imperative of never compromising the rights and dignity of individuals, regardless of the challenges they face. It also highlights the ongoing commitment to providing the most humane and effective treatments for mental disorders.

16. Moral Confinement

Among interventions and practices in the annals of mental health care history, we find "moral treatment." This was a significant milestone, representing a shift toward more humane care for individuals with mental illness. While it marked progress, it is now seen as outdated due to its limitations. The story of moral confinement provides valuable insights into the complex evolution of mental health care.

The concept of moral treatment emerged in the late 18th century as a response to the deplorable conditions in asylums and institutions where individuals with mental illness were often confined. Prior to the adoption of moral treatment, individuals suffering from psychiatric conditions were frequently subjected to harsh and inhumane conditions. They were often chained, shackled, and left to languish in squalid and overcrowded facilities.

Moral treatment was a reaction to these abhorrent practices, advocating for a more humane approach to the care of individuals with mental illness. It was grounded in the belief that a structured and supportive environment, combined with understanding and compassion, could aid in the recovery and rehabilitation of individuals with psychiatric conditions.

The central tenets of moral treatment included respect for individual dignity, the provision of a structured and supportive environment, the cultivation of therapeutic relationships, and the promotion of occupational therapy. One of the central tenets of moral treatment was the recognition of the inherent worth and dignity of individuals with mental illness. This marked a stark departure from the dehumanizing practices of the past.

Moral treatment emphasized the importance of providing individuals with a structured and therapeutic environment. This included access to clean and well-maintained facilities, as well as a daily routine that encouraged engagement in purposeful activities. Central to moral treatment was the belief that compassionate and therapeutic relationships between patients and caregivers were crucial for the recovery process. Caregivers were encouraged to provide emotional support and understanding to those under their care.

Moral treatment placed significant emphasis on occupational therapy and meaningful activities. Patients were encouraged to engage in productive work, such as gardening, sewing, or other crafts, as a means of promoting their well-being and self-esteem.

However, moral treatment was not without its limitations. It was primarily available to individuals from higher socio-economic backgrounds, leaving those without financial resources or social support at a disadvantage. Despite the significant improvements in conditions, confinement in institutions was still a fundamental aspect of the approach. The methods employed in moral treatment were based on compassionate care but lacked a solid scientific foundation. Treatment plans were often developed based on anecdotal evidence and clinical observations rather than rigorous scientific research. Additionally, there was a tendency to overestimate the effectiveness of moral treatment, as the belief in complete recovery and reintegration into society was unrealistic for many individuals with severe and persistent mental illnesses.

The emergence of the 20th century brought significant changes to the field of mental health care. Advances in psychiatry, the development of psychotropic medications, and a growing emphasis on empirical evidence led to a paradigm shift in the treatment of mental illness. Moral treatment began to decline as newer and more effective approaches emerged. The introduction of antipsychotic medications, psychotherapy, and community-based mental health care marked a significant departure from the institutionalization associated with moral treatment.

The legacy of moral treatment in the context of mental health care is a reflection of the evolving understanding of mental illness and shifting societal attitudes toward individuals with psychiatric conditions. While it may appear outdated and limited by contemporary standards, it was a significant step in the journey toward more humane and compassionate care for individuals with mental illness. It underscored the importance of treating individuals with respect and dignity and challenged the prevailing notion that individuals with mental illness were beyond help. The experiences of those who benefited from moral treatment are a testament to the potential for recovery and rehabilitation when individuals are provided with a supportive and structured environment. It is through empathy, understanding, and a commitment to evidence-based practices that mental health care has continued to evolve and improve. Today, the field of mental health care continues to advance, emphasizing the importance of evidence-based treatments, patient rights, and community-based care. While moral treatment may have had its limitations, it played a pivotal role in the ongoing quest for humane and effective treatments for mental illness.

17. Exorcism

Throughout history, diverse cultures have sought to understand and treat the complex manifestations of mental illness. In many ancient societies, such conditions were attributed to demonic possession, a belief that led to the practice of exorcism. These rituals were performed to expel the supposed evil spirits that were believed to cause this psychological and behavioral turmoil in individuals. The story of exorcism and its historical connection to mental illness is a profound illustration of humanity's enduring quest to confront the mysteries of the mind and the supernatural.

The concept of demonic possession has deep roots in ancient civilizations. In cultures across the world, people grappled with unexplainable behaviors, delusions, and altered states of consciousness. These perplexing experiences were often attributed to the influence of malevolent spirits or deities. The idea of being inhabited or controlled by such entities was a way to make sense of what was then poorly understood.

In many of these belief systems, it was believed that these malevolent spirits could take possession of an individual's body or mind, leading to what we now recognize as symptoms of mental illness. The afflicted individuals would often exhibit erratic behavior, hallucinations, and other signs of psychological distress. It was within this context that exorcism rituals emerged as an attempt to expel these perceived intruders and restore the individual's mental and emotional well-being.

Exorcism, as a therapeutic ritual, took various forms across different cultures and time periods. Common elements included the use of incantations, prayers, sacred objects, and the guidance of a religious or spiritual authority. The rituals were intended to evoke the supernatural, leading to the expulsion of the malevolent forces responsible for the individual's suffering.

These ceremonies were often highly symbolic, with the afflicted person representing a battleground where the forces of good and evil clashed. The exorcist, typically a religious figure, acted as a conduit for divine intervention. The hope was that through these rituals, the afflicted individual would be freed from the grip of the malevolent spirit and experience relief from their psychological torment.

In the context of exorcism, religion and spirituality played a central role. The rituals were deeply rooted in the belief systems of the time, and religious authorities were often the ones called upon to perform these ceremonies. It was believed that their connection to the divine made them uniquely qualified to confront and banish malevolent forces. The presence of religion and spirituality in exorcism underscored the profound interplay between the supernatural and the human experience. People sought solace and explanation in their faith, and exorcism provided a way to bridge the perceived gap between the sacred and the profane.

Over time, as scientific understanding advanced and the field of psychiatry emerged, perceptions of mental illness began to shift. The once widespread belief in demonic possession as the primary cause of psychiatric conditions started to wane. Instead, individuals with mental health issues were increasingly seen as individuals suffering from internal imbalances, neurological conditions, or psychological distress, rather than as vessels for malevolent spirits. The rise of modern medicine and the development of psychiatric treatments, such as psychotherapy and psychopharmacology, provided more evidence-based approaches to addressing mental illness. These advancements diminished the need for exorcism as a treatment method.

The legacy of exorcism in the context of mental illness is a testament to the evolving understanding of the human mind and the supernatural. While exorcism may seem like an archaic and irrational practice when viewed through a contemporary lens, it was once a sincere attempt to grapple with the enigma of mental illness. The experiences of those who underwent exorcism and the practitioners who performed these rituals are a reminder of the profound challenges that mental illness has posed throughout history. The belief in demonic possession and the practice of exorcism were, in part, born out of desperation, as ancient societies sought explanations and solutions for conditions that were poorly understood.

Today, our understanding of mental illness is grounded in the principles of empirical evidence, scientific research, and a holistic approach to mental health care. The development of psychiatric treatments and a greater awareness of the psychological and neurological underpinnings of mental illness have greatly improved our ability to support individuals who are grappling with these conditions.

The story of exorcism and its historical connection to mental illness underscores the enduring human quest to comprehend and confront the complex interplay of the mind and the supernatural. While we have come a long way in our understanding and treatment of mental illness, we must approach the topic with empathy, cultural sensitivity, and a recognition of the historical complexities that have shaped our perceptions of mental health.

18. Bloodletting

Throughout the annals of history, various cultures have grappled with the enigma of mental disturbances and their mysterious origins. In some of these societies, it was believed that such afflictions were caused by an excess of "bad blood" within the body, leading to practices of bloodletting in an attempt to remove the presumed impurities. The story of bloodletting and its historical association with the treatment of mental disturbances offers an intriguing glimpse into the evolution of medical practices and the enduring quest to understand and address complex mental conditions.

The practice of bloodletting can be traced back to ancient civilizations, including the Egyptians, Greeks, and Romans. It was grounded in the theory of the four humors, an ancient medical concept. According to this theory, the body's health and temperament were influenced by the balance of four humors: blood, phlegm, black bile, and yellow bile. Mental disturbances were often attributed to an imbalance in these humors, particularly an excess of "bad blood." It was believed that removing this tainted blood from the body would restore balance and alleviate psychological distress.

Bloodletting was performed using a variety of methods and tools, depending on the cultural and historical context. Common techniques included venesection, leeching, and cupping. Venesection involved making incisions in a vein to allow the blood to flow out. It was typically performed on veins located in the arms, and the amount of blood extracted varied depending on the patient's condition and the beliefs of the practitioner.

Alternatively, leeches were applied to the patient's skin, typically on the arms, legs, or neck. The leeches would attach themselves and feed on the patient's blood. Leeching was considered a more controlled method of bloodletting and was often used in cases where precise blood volume reduction was desired. In cupping, heated glass or metal cups were placed on the patient's skin to create a vacuum. This caused blood to be drawn to the surface, and small incisions were sometimes made to enhance the flow.

Bloodletting was a common medical practice not only for the treatment of mental disturbances but also for a wide range of other ailments, from fever to various physical illnesses. Practitioners believed that by regulating the balance of humors, the patient's overall health could be restored.

Bloodletting practices and beliefs varied significantly across cultures and time periods. For instance, in ancient Greece, the father of medicine, Hippocrates, supported the practice of bloodletting. He believed that it could be a beneficial treatment for a range of conditions, including mental disorders. In contrast, in ancient China, bloodletting was not commonly practiced, and traditional Chinese medicine focused on balancing the body's vital energies, or qi. Mental disturbances were often attributed to disturbances in the flow of qi. Consequently, treatments such as acupuncture and herbal remedies were employed to address these imbalances.

The practice of bloodletting persisted through the Middle Ages and into the Renaissance, with variations in techniques and cultural beliefs. In Europe, for example, it was commonly employed for a wide range of ailments, including mental disturbances.

As medical knowledge advanced and empirical evidence became more valued, the practice of bloodletting gradually began to wane. In the late 19th and early 20th centuries, bloodletting was largely discredited as a medical intervention. The development of modern psychiatry, alongside breakthroughs in neuroscience and the understanding of mental health conditions, brought about a significant shift in the approach to mental disturbances. The focus turned from the removal of bodily fluids to the treatment of the underlying psychological and neurological factors contributing to these conditions.

Antipsychotic medications, psychotherapy, and other evidence-based treatments emerged as more effective alternatives for addressing mental health disorders. The understanding of mental illness shifted from being rooted in the concept of humors and blood imbalances to a more holistic perspective that considers psychological, social, and biological factors.

The legacy of bloodletting in the context of mental disturbances highlights the evolution of medical practices and the quest for effective treatments for complex conditions. While bloodletting may appear antiquated and irrational through a contemporary lens, it was a sincere attempt to confront the challenges posed by mental disorders. The experiences of individuals who underwent bloodletting, as well as the practitioners who administered these treatments, offer a glimpse into the historical complexities surrounding mental health care. Bloodletting was practiced with the intention of alleviating suffering, even though it was rooted in a belief system that now seems archaic.

The story of bloodletting and its historical association with the treatment of mental disturbances serves as a reminder of the need for ongoing advancements in our understanding and treatment of mental health conditions. The lessons from this historical practice underscore the importance of empathy, evidence-based care, and the evolving nature of medical knowledge in the field of mental health. We have left behind the practice of bloodletting, but the ongoing quest for effective treatments for mental disturbances continues, grounded in contemporary understanding and the principles of compassionate care.

19. Trephination

Trephination is one of the most ancient and enduring. Also known as trepanation or trepanning, this procedure involves the removal of a circular piece of bone from the skull. Throughout history, it has been employed for a wide range of purposes, from the treatment of medical conditions to religious and ritualistic practices. The story of trephination offers a fascinating journey into the evolution of medical practices and the enduring quest to understand and heal the human body and mind.

The roots of trephination extend far back into human history, reaching across continents and civilizations. Archaeological evidence suggests that this practice was performed as early as the Neolithic period, approximately 10,000 years ago. Skulls with carefully made openings, likely created by trephination, have been discovered in various parts of the world, including Europe, the Americas, and Africa.

The motivations for trephination were diverse and multifaceted. In some cases, it was carried out as a medical intervention to address specific conditions, such as head injuries, skull fractures, or intracranial hemorrhages. In others, trephination held deep religious and cultural significance, serving as a ritualistic act aimed at achieving spiritual insights, releasing malevolent forces, or honoring the deceased.

Trephination was performed using a set of specialized tools that were painstakingly crafted from stone, bone, or metal. The location of the skull where the trephination would be performed was carefully chosen. It was crucial to avoid critical blood vessels and sensitive brain regions. A circular or oval incision was made on the selected site of the skull using a sharp tool, such as an obsidian blade. The surgeon needed to apply controlled pressure to avoid damaging the underlying brain.

Once the incision was complete, a piece of bone was carefully removed. This was achieved through a combination of skill, precision, and knowledge of the cranial anatomy. After the procedure, the wound was treated with various substances, such as clay or plant extracts, and the patient's head was bandaged to protect against infection. Healing could take weeks, and the patient was closely monitored during this time.

The motivations behind trephination varied significantly across different cultures and time periods. In some societies, it was predominantly a medical procedure aimed at addressing specific head injuries, fractures, or conditions causing increased intracranial pressure. For instance, in ancient Greece, the practice was used to treat head injuries and relieve the symptoms of hydrocephalus.

In other cases, trephination was driven by deeply rooted cultural and religious beliefs. In pre-Columbian Mesoamerica, the Maya and other civilizations practiced trephination as part of complex rituals. These rituals were thought to provide a bridge between the physical and spiritual worlds, granting those who underwent trephination access to divine knowledge and experiences.

The motivations for trephination in ancient cultures were as diverse as the cultures themselves. Among the reasons cited for this procedure were the release of evil spirits, the treatment of migraines, and the belief that it could provide spiritual insight. In some cultures, trephination was associated with tribal initiation rites, while in others, it was part of rituals to honor the deceased.

The enduring nature of trephination throughout human history is a testament to the cultural and medical significance it held in various societies. The practice continued into the medieval period and was employed in the treatment of head injuries resulting from combat or accidents. During this time, the role of the trepanator, or the individual who performed trephinations, was highly regarded, and they often held prominent positions within the community.

Even as the field of medicine advanced, with the development of surgical techniques and the emergence of modern neurosurgery, trephination did not entirely vanish. Some isolated cases of trephination have been reported in the 19th and 20th centuries, often as a last resort when no other medical treatment was available.

The legacy of trephination in the context of medical history is multifaceted and offers unique insights into the evolution of surgical practices and the beliefs surrounding the human body and mind. The history of trephination demonstrates the human drive to explore and understand the mysteries of the brain and its connection to health and well-being. In the modern era, our understanding of neurosurgery, brain anatomy, and the complexities of mental health has come a long way. Advances in medical science and technology have enabled us to diagnose and treat a wide range of neurological conditions with a level of precision and safety that was unimaginable in the past.

The story of trephination also reminds us of the cultural and spiritual significance that medical practices held in various societies. The intersection of medicine, ritual, and belief systems shaped the landscape of ancient healing practices, and trephination serves as a compelling example of this interplay. Today, the field of medicine is guided by evidence-based practices, ethical standards, and a commitment to patient well-being. Trephination, with its blend of medical and ritualistic purposes, offers a poignant reflection on the evolution of healthcare. It highlights the importance of evidence, safety, and respect for the patient's dignity.

The enduring practice of trephination, spanning millennia and continents, provides a unique window into the complexities of human history, culture, and medical evolution. While it may seem archaic by modern standards, the legacy of trephination serves as a poignant reminder of the human quest for knowledge and healing. It reflects the need to understand the intricate relationship between the mind, the body, and the spirit.

20. Electroconvulsive Therapy (ECT)

ECT was a medical treatment that has generated a wide range of opinions and emotions over the decades. It stands as one of the most enduring and controversial interventions in the history of mental health care. While ECT, in its modern form, remains a valuable tool for treating severe mental illnesses, its early incarnations were marred by crude methods that involved inducing seizures in patients through the application of electrical currents. The story of ECT is a journey through the shifting landscape of mental health care. It is marked by evolving practices and ethical considerations that continue to spark debates even today.

The origins of ECT can be traced back to the 1930s, when Italian neurologist Ugo Cerletti and his colleague Lucio Bini were inspired by observing the seizures of pigs during slaughtering. They hypothesized that inducing controlled seizures in patients might have therapeutic benefits for individuals with severe mental illnesses. This notion marked the birth of ECT as a medical procedure.

Early experiments with ECT involved the application of electrical currents to the temples of patients. The resulting seizures were often severe, leading to violent convulsions and the risk of physical injury. These early practices were largely unrefined and ethically questionable. In the mid-20th century, ECT gained notoriety as a treatment for severe mental illnesses, particularly in cases of severe depression and schizophrenia. During this period, ECT was often administered without the patient's informed consent, and its use was sometimes associated with institutionalization and societal stigmatization.

The procedure itself involved the administration of electrical shocks through electrodes placed on the patient's head. The induced seizures were characterized by violent convulsions, which sometimes resulted in fractures, dental damage, and other physical injuries. The early ECT was, by modern standards, a crude and harsh treatment. Over time, ECT underwent significant refinements in both technique and ethical considerations. The field of psychiatry began to recognize the importance of informed consent, patient safety, and the minimization of discomfort and adverse effects.

In modern ECT, the procedure is performed in a controlled and monitored environment. Anesthesia and muscle relaxants are administered to ensure that the patient does not experience the violent convulsions of the past. Electrodes are carefully placed on the patient's head, and a precisely controlled electrical current is applied to induce a seizure that is typically much milder than the early convulsions.

The modern ECT is often used as a treatment of last resort for severe mental illnesses, such as treatment-resistant depression, bipolar disorder, and schizophrenia. It has been found to be effective in some cases where other interventions have failed. It is typically administered in a series of sessions under the guidance of a trained medical team.

ECT remains a topic of significant controversy and ethical debate, even in its modern form. Critics argue that the procedure still lacks comprehensive research to fully understand its mechanisms and potential long-term effects. Concerns have been raised about memory loss, both retrograde (loss of past memories) and anterograde (difficulty forming new memories), as a potential side effect of ECT. The use of ECT without informed consent, as was common in the mid-20th century, has left a lasting scar on the procedure's reputation. Advocates for patient rights emphasize the importance of comprehensive informed consent and the option for alternative treatments. They argue that ECT should be considered a choice, rather than a mandated treatment.

The controversy surrounding ECT reflects the ongoing tension between the potential benefits of the procedure in treating severe mental illnesses and the ethical concerns regarding safety, consent, and potential side effects.

Despite the controversy, ECT continues to be utilized in the treatment of severe mental illnesses. It is often considered when other interventions, including medication and psychotherapy, have proven ineffective. The decision to use ECT is typically made by a team of mental health professionals, and it is accompanied by a thorough informed consent process. Research on the effectiveness of ECT has shown positive outcomes for certain patients. It can provide rapid relief from severe depression and suicidal ideation. Some individuals with treatment-resistant mental illnesses have experienced significant improvement in their symptoms, enabling them to resume their daily lives.

As the field of mental health care continues to evolve, the ethical imperative in the use of ECT remains a critical consideration. Modern medical and ethical guidelines underscore the importance of patient autonomy, informed consent, and safety. Patient experiences and preferences should be central to the decision-making process. The controversies and debates surrounding ECT reflect the broader complexities of mental health care. They highlight the ongoing need for research, open dialogue, and the ethical treatment of individuals with severe mental illnesses.

The story of ECT represents the enduring dialogue within the field of mental health care. While modern ECT has evolved to become a safer and more controlled procedure, it remains the subject of ethical debates and critical reflection. The practice of ECT is a reminder of the evolving landscape of mental health care and the challenges that persist in balancing the potential benefits of treatments with the ethical concerns that surround them.

The ongoing dialogue about ECT testify to the commitment of the mental health community to seek the most effective and ethical approaches to treating severe mental illnesses. In the end, the story of ECT is a story of hope and healing, but also one that highlights the need for compassion, ethical consideration, and the continuous pursuit of understanding and improving the treatment of severe mental illnesses.

Conclusion

As we draw the final curtain on this exploration of historical interventions for mental illnesses, we find ourselves at the intersection of time, where the past meets the present. The journey we embarked upon has taken us through a fascinating landscape of beliefs, practices, and ethical considerations that have shaped the way society has understood and addressed mental illness.

From the dark specter of exorcism, where mental disturbances were attributed to demonic possession and individuals sought solace in the rituals of expulsion, to the curious world of mesmerism, where magnets and hypnosis were used to heal, we have traversed a spectrum of approaches that ranged from the bizarre to the compassionate.

We witnessed the curious science of phrenology, which claimed to unveil personality traits through the study of skull contours, and the early days of psychosurgery, where frontal lobotomies left a legacy of ethical quandaries. We uncovered the paradox of moral confinement, which, though well-intentioned, marked a chapter in history when individuals with mental illnesses found themselves restricted within structured environments.

We explored the extremes of medical practices, from bloodletting to forced vomiting, blistering, and tranquilizer chairs, each an attempt to bring balance and healing to the complexities of the human mind. The eerie specter of insulin-induced comas and the once-hailed practice of blood transfusions illuminated the uncertainty and evolving nature of psychiatric treatments. The ancient procedure of trephination, with its cultural and ritualistic implications, revealed the remarkable resilience of the human spirit and the enduring quest to transcend the boundaries of the mind.

Finally, the evolution of electroconvulsive therapy (ECT) from its early, crude forms to the refined, ethical treatment it is today, signifies a bridge between past and present. It exemplifies the commitment of the mental health community to adapt, improve, and navigate the complex interplay of science, ethics, and human suffering.

As we take leave of these pages, we do so with a deep appreciation for the complexity of the human experience. The journey through these historical interventions for mental illness reminds us that our understanding of the mind and its ailments is a continually evolving narrative. Our commitment to compassionate, effective, and ethical care persists through time.

The past has bequeathed us a legacy of trial and error, where often cruel and misguided interventions have existed alongside well-intentioned practices. This rich tapestry of history serves as a mirror in which we can reflect on the present and look towards the future.

In this concluding chapter, we recognize the indomitable spirit of humanity, which has persisted in the face of adversity. It continues forging onward in the pursuit of understanding, healing, and compassion. It is a testament to the resilience of the human spirit that even in times when understanding was limited and practices were flawed, individuals sought solace and relief for those who bore the heavy burden of mental illness.

As we close the book on this chapter of history, we acknowledge the significant progress made in the field of mental health care. Today, scientific research, ethical guidelines, and evidence-based practices guide the care of individuals experiencing mental illness. The lessons learned from the past interventions underscore the importance of continuous improvement, empathy, and the ethical treatment of those in need.

The story of these interventions is not a mere recounting of bygone practices. It is a testament to the enduring commitment of humanity to confront and understand the intricate challenges posed by mental disorders. It is a chronicle of the human spirit's unyielding determination to extend a compassionate hand to those grappling with the shadows of the mind.

In the end, we emerge from these pages with a deeper understanding of the past and a renewed dedication to improving the present and shaping a future where mental health care is guided by science, ethics, and the profound belief that healing is possible. This journey through the ages of mental health interventions is a reminder of the enduring human quest for understanding, compassion, and the alleviation of suffering. It is a journey that continues to shape the course of history and the well-being of countless lives.

References

1. Bleed, Blister, Puke, and Purge: The Dirty Secrets Behind Early American Medicine by J. Marin Younker (2019). Lerner Publishing Group.

2. Cahoon, H. (1949). The Pre-frontal Lobotomy as a Treatment for Mental Illness. United States: (n.p.).

3. Combe, G. (1819). Essays on Phrenology; Or, An Inquiry Into the Principles and Utility of the System of Drs. Gall and Spurzheim, and Into the Objections Made Against it. Bell & Bradfute, Edinburgh, and Longman, Hurst, Rees, Orme & Browne, London.

4. Concordia University. (2020, July 13). A History of Mental Illness Treatment: Obsolete Practices. Retrieved from
https://online.csp.edu/resources/article/history-of-mental-illness-treatment/

5. Earle, P. (1854). An Examination of the Practice of Bloodletting in Mental Disorders. United States: Wood.

6. Geller, M. R. (1962). The Treatment of Psychiatric Disorders with Insulin: 1936-1960; a Selected Annotated Bibliography. Compiled for the Psychopharmacology Service Center, National Institute of Mental Health, National Institutes of Health. United States: U. S. Department of Health, Education, and Welfare, Public Health Service.

7. Geller, M. R. (1963). The Treatment of Psychiatric Disorders with Metrazol (Volume 39). U.S. Department of Health, Education, and Welfare, Public Health Service.

8. Gross, C. G. (2012). A Hole in the Head: More Tales in the History of Neuroscience. United Kingdom: MIT Press.

9. Haycock, W. (2000). Osteopathy Principles & Practice • Volume 2. Institute of Classical Osteopathy.

10. LAbate, L. (2012). Mental Illnesses: Understanding, Prediction, and Control. IntechOpen.

11. McCasland, S. V. (1951). By the Finger of God: Demon Possession and Exorcism in Early Christianity in the Light of Modern Views of Mental Illness. United States: Macmillan.

12. National Institute of Mental Health (U.S.). (1973). Psychosurgery: Perspectives on a Current Problem. U.S. Department of Health, Education, and Welfare, Health Services and Mental Health Administration, National Institute of Mental Health.

13. Noll, R. (2009). The Encyclopedia of Schizophrenia and Other Psychotic Disorders. Facts On File, Incorporated.

14. N.A. (1843). The Phrenological Journal. Simpkin, Marshall, and Company.

15. Porter, R. (2007). Medicine, Madness and Social History: Essays in Honour of Roy Porter. United Kingdom: Palgrave Macmillan.

16. Rush, B. (1794). Medical Inquiries and Observations on the Diseases of the Mind (5th ed.). Thomas Dobson.

17. Shorter, E., Healy, D. (2007). Shock Therapy: A History of Electroconvulsive Treatment in Mental Illness. United Kingdom: Rutgers University Press.

18. The Confinement of the Insane: International Perspectives, 1800–1965. (2003). (n.p.): Cambridge University Press.

19. U.S. Department of Health, Education and Welfare, Public Health Service, Alcohol, Drug Abuse and Mental Health Administration. (1977). Schizophrenia Bulletin.

20. Welton, T., Fryar, R. H. (1884). Mental Magic: A Rationale of Thought Reading and Its Attendant Phenomena and Their Application to the Discovery of New Medicines, Obscure Diseases, Correct Delineations of Character, Lost Persons and Property, Mines and Springs of Water, and All Hidden and Secret Things. United Kingdom: G. Redway.